Your Momma Thinks Square Roots Are Vegetables

Other FoxTrot Books by Bill Amend

FoxTrot • Pass the Loot • Black Bart Says Draw • Eight Yards, Down and Out
Bury My Heart at Fun-Fun Mountain • Say Hello to Cactus Flats • May the Force Be with Us, Please
Take Us to Your Mall • The Return of the Lone Iguana • At Least This Place Sells T-shirts
Come Closer, Roger, There's a Mosquito on Your Nose • Welcome to Jasorassic Park
I'm Flying, Jack . . . I Mean, Roger • Think iFruity • Death by Field Trip
Encyclopedias Brown and White • His Code Name Was The Fox

Anthologies

FoxTrot: The Works • FoxTrot *en masse* • Enormously FoxTrot • Wildly FoxTrot
FoxTrot Beyond a Doubt • Camp FoxTrot • Assorted FoxTrot • FoxTrot: Assembled with Care

Your Momma Thinks Square Roots Are Vegetables

A FoxTrot Collection
by Bill Amend

Andrews McMeel
Publishing

Kansas City

———————— **ATTENTION: SCHOOLS AND BUSINESSES** ————————

Andrews McMeel books are available at quantity discounts with bulk purchase for educational, business, or sales promotional use. For information, please write to: Special Sales Department, Andrews McMeel Publishing, 4520 Main Street, Kansas City, Missouri 64111.

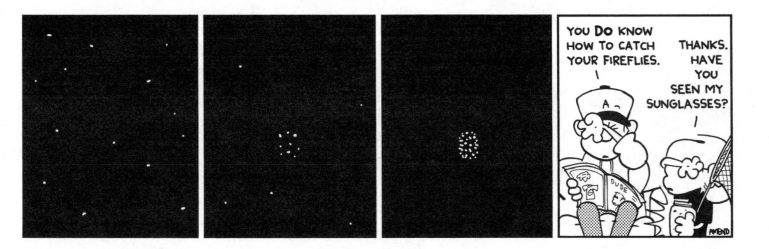

18

FOR AS LONG AS I CAN REMEMBER, DAD'S ALWAYS BEEN AFRAID OF SHOTS AND NEEDLES.

AND YET HE WENT OUT AND DONATED BLOOD THIS WEEK ANYWAY.

WOULD I BE TOO BIG A GEEK IF I WENT AND TOLD HIM I WAS PROUD OF HIM?

THIS FROM A KID WHO WEARS BOBA FETT UNDERPANTS.

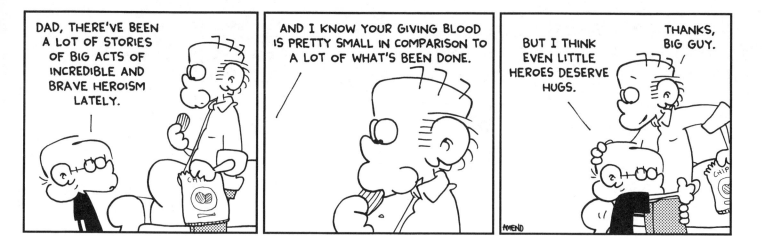

DAD, THERE'VE BEEN A LOT OF STORIES OF BIG ACTS OF INCREDIBLE AND BRAVE HEROISM LATELY.

AND I KNOW YOUR GIVING BLOOD IS PRETTY SMALL IN COMPARISON TO A LOT OF WHAT'S BEEN DONE.

BUT I THINK EVEN LITTLE HEROES DESERVE HUGS.

THANKS, BIG GUY.

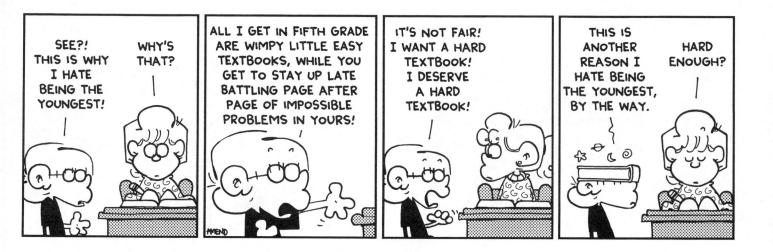

33

34

39

40

42

43

44

53

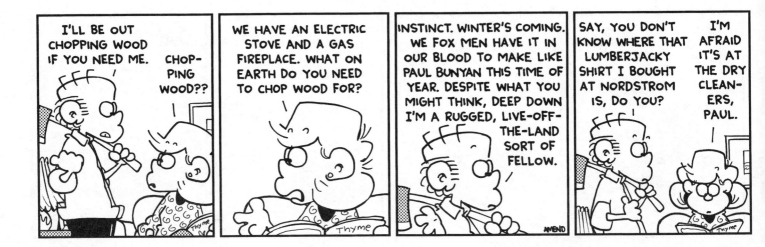

58

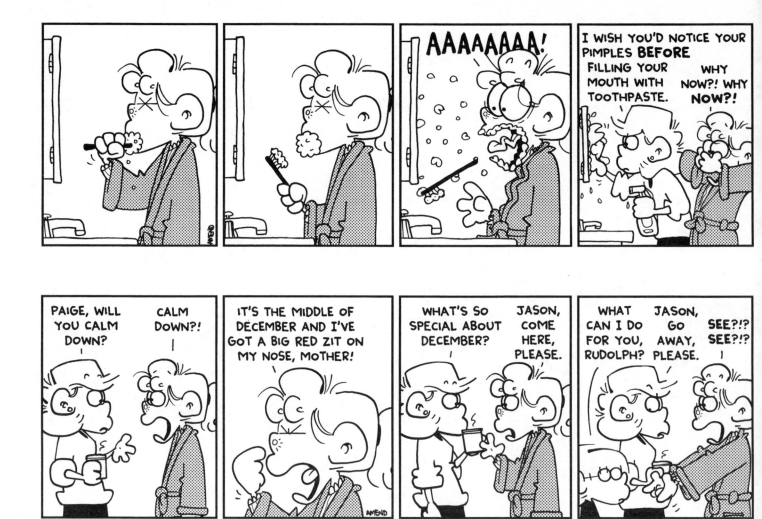

65

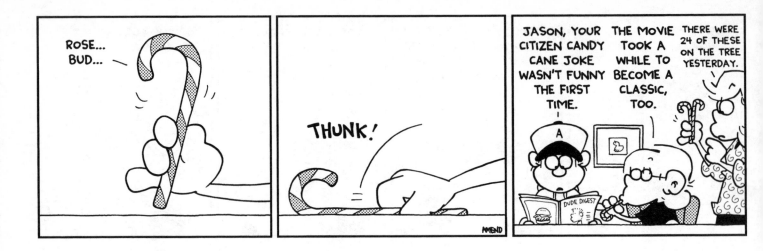

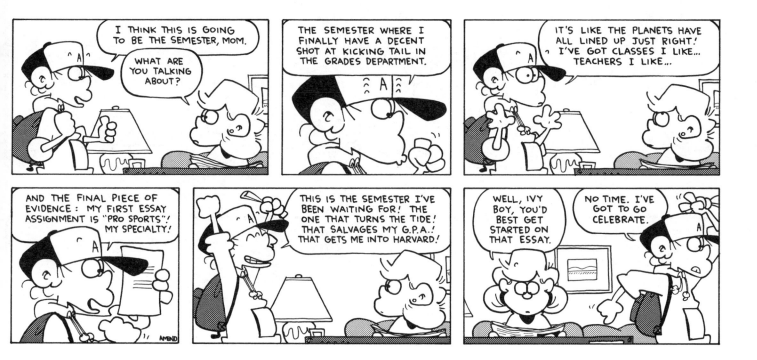

83

86

88

89

LET THE JASON AND MARCUS WINTER GAMES COMMENCE!
FIRST EVENT: CROSS-COUNTRY SKEDADDLING.
AMEND

YOU KNOW, UPHILL RACING WOULD BE A COOL SPORT, TOO.
THEY'D HAVE TO DO BLOOD TESTS FOR HELIUM, THOUGH.
AMEND

113

114

115

120

125